From Afar, I Hold You Close

Poems on Love, Loss, and Spaces In Between

Bhavesh Boyal

BookLeaf Publishing

India | USA | UK

Made with ❤ on the BookLeaf Publishing Platform
www.bookleafpub.in
www.bookleafpub.com

Dedication

To my family—

To my mother and father, who have given me love, freedom, and above all, a life they never truly lived but let me live. Your sacrifices, silent yet immense, have shaped my every step.

And to my sister, my unwavering pillar of strength, whose belief in me has been a light in my darkest days. Your words have been my refuge, your support my greatest gift.

This book is but a small tribute to the love that has made me who I am.

Preface

Poetry, to me, is life itself—fluid, boundless, and ever-unfolding. Life is a poem written in moments, felt in heartbeats. Poetry is the history of the human soul, etched in words that time cannot erase.

This collection of poems, From Afar, I Hold You Close , delves into the complexities of human connections—the unspoken words, the fleeting moments, and the emotions that linger long after. Through these verses, I hope to capture the beauty and heartbreak of bonds that shape us, like whispers in the wind, forever felt but never quite held.

Acknowledgements

I extend my sincere gratitude to BookLeaf Publications for providing me with the perfect platform to embark on my journey as a writer. Their 21-day challenge was exactly the opportunity I was looking for to turn my passion into reality. This experience has been both enriching and inspiring, and I truly appreciate their support in making my debut as an author possible.

Thank you for this incredible initiative!

Scent of her Soul

I found a soul,
Not ordinary, not just a dream.
A woman of grace, mature and serene,
Beautiful beyond what eyes have seen.

She wasn't like the rest,
Chasing a fleeting label.
She sought a love that felt like home,
A heart steadfast, true, and stable.

Someone to hold her hand,
From daylight bird songs to midnight stars.
A love that lingers in whispered winds,
Unshaken by time or scars.

I love her truly, with all my soul,
Her presence makes my heart feel whole.
Her bushy brows, her fragrant hair,
And that smile like a whisper only the heart can bear.

It's been so long since I last saw her,
Yet she lives in every word I weave.
If these words find you, my love,
Would you return to kiss me once?

Hey, Oh! Stranger!

Hey, Oh! Stranger!
They say you're fine,
so they never ask twice.

But I see you—
lost in the noise,
hiding in plain sight.

Are you pretending again?
Drifting with no shore?

Just know, love,
you are enough,
right here,
right now.

Two Stubborn Hearts

Yes, I walked away.
Leaving you with nothing but a hollow excuse.
I was a fool, who can't admit when he's sorry.
Maybe now, I'm just a name you never speak.

Yes, I regret it.
I stand at our place,
And there's no one to blame.
And I miss the shape of your lips.
Lost in a battle where no one won—
just two stubborn hearts,
too fierce to surrender,
too fragile to last.

Between Tears and Smile

Today, something peculiar happened.
someone dear to me did.

We are all social animals,
Yet crave our inner peace.
When it shatters,
I do things I wouldn't.
I ask myself:
Is this really me?

"Try to understand their side," they say.
But why must it always be me?
"Leave them alone for now," they add.
Can we all open up before it's all too much?

I penned this while traveling in my car, Tears fell from
my eyes,
I painted them in hues of yellow,
And then, I smiled,
Perhaps,
That's life.

Double Tap, Empty Hands

you left,
but your shadow didn't.

you don't text,
but your name stays at the top of my story views,
lingering like nicotine,
i know you're bad for me,
but you still linger in my lungs.

i post my coffee,
you double tap—nothing more.

if you wanted to be here,
you would be.
but all you do is orbit,
and i'm done looking up.

Unfinished Kisses

He holds your hand, but not too tight,
Keeps you close, then leaves your sight.

A game he plays—you always know,

Yet still, you stay, yet still, you hope.

You love a fool who plays it smart,

But never lets you have his heart.

Just like this poem, the bond fades in pieces,

Leaving behind only unfinished kisses.

If you stay... If you go...

Let the heart settle,
How do I stop you from leaving?

Stay a moment, don't walk away,
Let my heart find words to say.
With you, the pain just drifts apart,
Like waves that calm a restless heart.

I see your dreams, they shine so bright,
Yet somewhere in them, hides the night.
Words of love, or mere disguise?
A gentle touch, or a web of lies?

If you stay, the rose will bloom in red.
If you go, the petals fall, love dead.

If you stay, the sun will rise,
If you go, so will my skies...

The Poetry in Me

I am a traveler, always gone,
Barely return, once or twice to home.

I miss my city, my childhood days,
Yet comfort feels like a cage that stays.

I walk with strangers, new stories to tell,
No past to haunt, no judgment to dwell.

I chase the world, the endless skies,
Yet some nights, a whisper cries—

Come back home, just for a while,
Let the road rest, let the heart smile.

The Funeral of my Wife

Thursday, October 31st.

Today, Is the funeral of my wife.
And I stand before her body.
Her eyes are wide open,
Her lips, dry as autumn leaves.
Yet, our wedding ring still rests on her finger.

The priest is about to do the homily,
But I have no words for my grief.

The air is colder than it should be,
too soon for the season.
Mourning faces surround me—
my mother, my children, her parents.
I'm sad too,
They whisper, "*I'm sorry for your loss.*"
But not all losses just happen—
some are made.

Softer Than Goodbyes

We didn't end, we just became
a softer thing, a gentler name.

Not lovers now, but something true,
a quiet bond, a different hue.

No bitter words, no closing doors,
just friendship growing, nothing more.

something steady, something kind,
something softer than goodbyes.

Sweet Creature

she called me an creature,
said my spine curled like a question mark,
my neck stiff as a stubborn door,

"*Your skin!*", she laughed,
like an old leather jacket left out in the rain.
"*Your hair!*" she smirked,
like a rare species—endangered, yet holding on.

Creature, creature, creature!

she pulled me closer,
then asked,
"*How much sugar do you want in your coffcc?*"

Wounded Soul

Wounded soul,
I know you're tired of pretending,
brushing off the hurt like it was never there.
You tie up your hair, force a smile—
like it's no big deal.

Wounded soul,
Your childhood echoes in your heart,
Silent scars that never fade,
Whispering fears, reminding you—
That love, sometimes, comes too late.

Wounded soul,
I know you're scarred, so am I.
A piece of you feels lost,
We may not know the cure,
But a hug can help us heal for sure

Expanding masculinity

Strong, unshaken—that's the way,
But must it be the only way?
Bravery shines in war and more,
But pride must not make men soar.

For years, the same old norms we see,
How about expanding masculinity?

Long hair flows, bold and free,
Beauty's not just her or me.
Pink's not just a woman's hue,
Nail paint shines on men too.

Clothes don't define love or desire,
Wear what you want, reach even higher.

Let all live full, no judgment, no fight,
Not above, not below—just equal in light.

Without Words, Love Withers

He walked with her through silent nights,
A steady flame in fading lights.
His care was soft, his heart was pure,
But words unspoken, hearts unsure.

One day she sighed, her voice so bare,
"You care too much, it's hard to bear."
He asked her why, but she withdrew,
A love once strong now split in two.

She came back, her voice was weak,
"Is this the price for all I seek?" he said.
She tried her view, but it was too late,
He stood as stiff as stone, no room for fate.

For love craves more than gestures kind,
It seeks the soul, the heart, the mind.
For deeds alone can't bridge the space,
If souls don't speak, love fades in place.

You Still Have Me

It was our 71st anniversary.
I was writing a poem for her—
the one thing that still made her happy, after our son.
I didn't know what was coming next.

My son walked in.
"There's an urgent meeting. We can't celebrate today." he
said.
Those were the only words he spoke to me.
Not even a wish.

A quiet ache settled in my chest.
What's the point of celebration if there is no family?
I couldn't face her.
So, I stepped outside.

I found myself at the old seashore—
where our love once began.
I was alone.
And then, a familiar warmth.

Her hand held mine.
"It's okay, You still have me." she whispered.

Maybe, in the end, that's all that truly matters.

Serendipity

They walked the same streets, stood in the same places,
but never at the same time.
Moments slipped by unnoticed,
like whispers in a crowded room.

One day, a lost wallet.
Familiar handwriting on an old ID.
A childhood friend, a name that felt like home.
Memories rushed in, unfinished, waiting.

Some stories pause, not end.
Time folds in unexpected ways.
What was lost was never really gone—
it was only waiting to be found.

The Cycle of Broken Hearts

He once loved true, but love betrayed,
Left him shattered, lost, afraid.
Now trust feels like a foolish game,
And love, to him, is just a name
.

Then someone came,
with love, so pure, so bright,
A beacon glowing in the night.
But blinded by his broken past,
He let her go—she loved her last.

Perhaps the one who broke him felt the same once,
don't you think?

The Unseen Horizon

A mid-January morning,
I stood at the cliff's edge—
Familiar, yet new.
A cold breeze traced my cheeks,
a distant train echoed,
birds hummed their secrets.
Frost kissed my fingers,
until the sun's warmth
gently held them.
I stepped closer—
but a hand pulled me back.
"Not here," my mother whispered.
As we drove away,
the birds kept singing.
Maybe someday, I will see them.

Your Voice, My Identity

You say I overreact,
that the echoes I hear are my own voice,
but the walls whisper back,
twisting my words,
until I no longer trust my own mind.

I tell you I'm tired,
that I just need a little space.

"You don't love me anymore, do you?"

Exhaustion fades into panic,
into the need to prove you wrong.

"You always push me away. Why do I even try?"

And just like that,
self-care becomes selfishness,
distance turns into betrayal.

I look in the mirror,
but the face staring back is unfamiliar.
"Who am I?" I whisper.

Your voice responds,
"Whoever I tell you to be."

Let Love Find You

They said love is out there, waiting to be found,
hidden in whispers, lost in the crowd.
But love is not a chase nor race,
it's the quiet joy of finding your place.

It's in the songs you sing for you,
in dreams pursued, in skies so blue.
Not borrowed, not begged, not chased, not sold—
but a fire inside, bright and bold.

So plant patience, water kindness,
let your roots run deep and wild.
One day, love may knock on your door,
but today, love lives right where you stand.

The Last Picture in Pushkar

I sat to write, but words felt stuck,
So I stepped outside, out of luck.
Home was silent, heavy, still—
A sorrow I could almost feel.

"*Jeetu is gone*," they softly said,
And something in me filled with dread.
Not just a driver, he was my past,
A childhood bond meant to last.

He never let a lens define,
Said memories live, not stay confined.
Yet once in Pushkar, he stood with me,
A single photo—our only memory.

Shattered, lost, I turned away,
Too numb to speak, too hurt to stay.

That night I wandered, where moonlight wept,
Chasing the echoes of a soul I'd kept.
The brightest star caught my eye,
Maybe it's him, at peace up high.

Father found me, saw my pain,

"*You miss him, don't you?*" he said again.

I asked, "*Where did he leave this world?*"

He simply whispered—

"*Pushkar.*"

www.ingramcontent.com/pod-product-compliance
Lightning Source LLC
Chambersburg PA
CBHW071242140726
47996CB00007B/2713